#ShazSays

The Love Series

Sharon Mukuze

ISBN: 9798842031306

DEDICATION

This book is dedicated to all those who believe in love after love.

ACKNOWLEDGMENTS

I would like to thank my brothers: Oscar, Gerald and Nila for believing in my dreams.

I cannot leave out my sister, Chipo and my friends, Swa, Nomsa, Charity, Patie, Thandi and Nettie with whom I shared a lot of my love stories.

A special thanks to my children Tawana, Tamara and Shannon (RIP) for showing me that I could love unconditionally.

This book would not have seen the light of day if it had not been for my friend and partner, Brian. Thank you for helping me share my thoughts with the world. Most of all, thank you for your love which matches mine.

PREFACE

Love is very beautiful yet the most misunderstood. A lot of times, people refer to love as something that's really messed up when they have been hurt by their significant others. Truth of the matter is, love is not what's messed up; it's us who are.

There are many facets of love and all which are important. We should try to understand each of these in order to really grasp the concept of love and/or that of our relationships. This will help us get the kind of attention we desire.

Relationships require a lot to keep them going and growing. Both parties have to be willing to put in the work otherwise one will be left hurt and wanting. Love is beautiful when it is mutual. Sadly, a lot of relationships lack this balance.

While love unifies two hearts, it is of utter importance that the two remain individuals. It's so easy (and beautiful) to love someone and get lost in the relationship. The danger comes when we lose ourselves in the process. This then breeds dependency issues.

This book seeks to empower the individual as well as the couple.

Enjoy…

The Love Series

If you find yourself doubting his love for you
then it probably doesn't exist.

#ShazSays

Have you ever been in a relationship with someone that makes you wonder whether or not they love you? Well, many of us have been. The truth is, if someone loves you, they will show and say it well enough for you to be secure in that regard. Don't be blinded by your love for them - they have to love you too.

****

Mature in friendship with your partner; it will help create a unique oneness.

#ShazSays

It is important to be friends with your partner. When you feel comfortable in someone else's space, it makes it easy for you to be expressive. Friendship in a relationship works wonders. It brings a certain level of fun and this helps in bonding.

****

Do it for her just coz it's a Thursday.

#ShazSays

Getting gifts on special days like anniversaries, birthdays, Christmas and so on is great, but the gifts that really count, are those random, unexpected ones.

****

Be the type of woman who brings a lot to the table. If he doesn't see it, then he's not the one.

#ShazSays

Over the years, there have been debates on what individuals should bring to the relationship and the importance thereof. What do you bring to the table? Looks and character, while important, are not of great or essential value to a relationship.

****

In the art of love, sexual chemistry is a great asset.

#ShazSays

Sex, sex and more sex! While sex is not the only form of intimacy, it is of essence. Sexual chemistry makes love-making/sex pleasurable. Well sexed partners are blissful - they glow.

****

Be with the one you wanna grow old and grey
with.

#ShazSays

What beauty is a relationship if it doesn't last! Even though things may go sideways, the intention should be to have the relationship last forever. If you do not see forever with them, then spare them.

****

In your relationship, crown each other.

#ShazSays

Supporting and celebrating each other is great
in a relationship. Honouring and respecting
each other is even greater.

****

Don't forget the simple things in life.

#ShazSays

Many times, people go out of their way to please their partners. While there is nothing wrong with this, it is equally important to maintain the simple things like taking walks, sitting happily in silence and so on.

****

Be consistent in being the man she fell in love with.

#ShazSays

If she has plans to stay and you don't want those plans to change, then be consistent in being the man she fell in love with. Men are hunters and they will stop at nothing to get what they want. The danger comes after they have caught their prey - they put their hunting game to sleep.

****

Let love be the foundation of it all. The magic
ain't in getting married but in staying married.

#ShazSays

The rate at which people are getting married is increasing. The divorce rate though, is alarming! People are getting married for all the wrong reasons. Love should be the foundation of the marriage institute coz love endures all things.

****

Ladies, stop holding on to the wrong man out
of fear of being alone.

#ShazSays

One thing you should know is that if he ain't right for you today, he ain't gon' be right for you tomorrow. Let go now and avoid investing in something that's not yours.

****

Enjoy love; don't cheat yourself. Love with all you've got. Remember, the experience is for you.

#ShazSays

Many times, because of heartbreaks, people tend to want to be safe from pain during the course of their relationship. Unfortunately, this doesn't work with love. The experience of love is for you. Enjoy it, withholding nothing.

****

Yes, say it but show it more. Action speaks louder than words.

#ShazSays

We have heard it said many times that action speaks louder than words and it's true. There is nothing more confusing than words that don't match the actions. When this happens, chose the message from the actions.

****

Only beautiful hearts can love.

#ShazSays

Have you ever heard people say that hurt people hurt people? Well, it's true. Love is usually a projection of what lies deep within the heart - it is difficult to fake. Open your eyes.

****

Great bonds are created in moments spent
together and in battles fought together.

#ShazSays

Quality time with your partner is essential in growing your relationship. The more time you spend together, the tighter your bond is most likely going to be. Now, when you go through and win battles together, your bond has a great chance of surviving even after a breakup.

****

Enjoy love in it's simplest form.

#ShazSays

At times we complicate things instead of keep them simple yet beautiful. Simple things like taking walks, staying in bed all day etc. have great potential in making a relationship very fruitful. What simple things can you think of? Make them a part of your relationship.

****

Take away all the doubt and fear and fall in
love again.

#ShazSays

Even after being hurt, heal and fall in love again. Your previous relationship may have made you question love but don't let it hinder you from enjoying the next one - it is not going to be the same.

****

Sometimes the person meant for you is right
in front of you.

#ShazSays

A lot of times people miss out on great potential relationships because they ignore the consistent person in front of them while focusing on someone they simply crush on yet never notices them. Open your eyes.

****

Sometimes you need to just silence your way
out of heartache.

#ShazSays

Have you ever been in a relationship where you clearly see that your partner's intentions are not pure? Sometimes it's not worth talking about. Just walk away.

****

The strength of a relationship is in being
friends first.

#ShazSays

The relationships I've seen to last are those in which friendship is built first. Taking time to know your partner and building on that is important. It will pay off in the long run.

****

Love is beautiful.

#ShazSays

Regardless of what people say or how people perceive love, it is beautiful. We miss it when we liken it to the people who hurt us. Search the true meaning of love and you will see how beautiful it is.

****

In your relationship, be careful not to fall in the trap of gradual erosion; gradual erosion of your passion. It is hard to get that back. Keep the fire burning.

#ShazSays

They say, "We just grew apart". There are many times when people relax during a relationship and neglect to make the effort to keep their connection strong. At times it happens in such subtle ways that can easily go unnoticed. This is a recipe for disaster. Keep cultivating the relationship.

****

Beautiful people and beautiful hearts make
love incredible.

#ShazSays

It makes no difference how much one can try to disguise it; a cruel heart can never love. The love from a beautiful heart cannot be compared to no other. The qualities of a beautiful heart match those of love. Nothing can beat this!

****

No matter how many times they broke your heart, love is not messed up; they are.

#ShazSays

Love is beautiful. If you find yourself
attracting the same kind of people or
relationships, then maybe it's time to evaluate
yourself. Do this before your pain rules out
the beauty of love.

****

Love is meant to be eternal. Make it last.

#ShazSays

I've seen a lot of marriages around me failing, well, including my first marriage. While the issues leading to these many divorces may vary, I still think, well, in my case at least, that the foundation may not have been love even though love was professed. Love goes beyond just the word love. We need to clearly understand it if our relationships are going to work.

****

While it's important to know where you stand in a relationship, just don't forget to enjoy love.

#ShazSays

There are times we find ourselves in a relationship before we even know a person's intentions. We meet, we connect and the relationship gets going. A little while later, we then want to try and figure out our partner's intentions. Guess what, it may just be too late. Just enjoy the relationship instead of always wanting to calculate things.

****

Be sure to know how your partner receives
love before you mourn about how they don't
appreciate your love.

#ShazSays

We tend to love people the way in which we understand love. There's nothing wrong with this. Only danger comes when we don't make an effort to find out how best our partner receives love. Have you ever heard couples argue about this? One says "you don't love me!" The other replies "I provide everything you want and need. You lack nothing! How can you say that I don't love you?"

This simply shows that one has been showering gifts etc. and yet maybe what was really needed was more time spent together. How do you receive love? How does your partner receive love?

****

Love is beautiful when it's mutual.

#ShazSays

A lot of the times when people are hurt, it is because they would have been in a relationship with someone who was just not that into them. Pain comes when we love but don't receive the love in return. This distorts the whole aspect of love. I hope you find someone who equally loves you.

****

Intimacy is not purely physical. It's the act of
connecting with someone so deeply that you
feel you can see into their soul.

#ShazSays

While the physical magic is great, connecting with someone emotionally and mentally is even greater. You may not even make love and yet still feel the connection. This kind of connection grows when two lovers take the time to get to know each other. After knowing each other, they purposely love each other while looking beyond the flaws. There is nothing that beats this kind of connection.

****

Let love lead.

#ShazSays

In everything we do, let love be what drives us. When we give, let love be what propels us. When we want to be with someone, let love be the reason. Even when we are having a disagreement, the desire to fix things should be driven by love. In all we do, let love lead.

****

If it was real then it won't end even when it ends.

#ShazSays

Have you ever been in a relationship with someone but somehow, the relationship fails? And even after things end, you still feel some form of love towards them… Well, I think it shows the love between you was real. You continue to love them even after you both move on. In as much as you may make the conscious decision to not go back to them, you still have a certain level of love for them. It just doesn't end…

****

Don't stop believing in love simply because it
didn't work out before.

#ShazSays

There are several reasons as to why a relationship may fail. A lot of the times we are left hurt and questioning a lot of things. When this happens, find healing and peace then open up your heart to love again. One man's mistakes don't make them the standard of every man. Give yourself to love again. It can only get better.

****

The beauty of any relationship is going through issues and overcoming them together. Weather the storm together.

#ShazSays

The friendships that we remain loyal to are with people we have weathered a storm (or many) with. There is a certain bond that's created from weathering storms together. Such is the case when we love someone. Fight together. Conquer together and the bond will be stronger.

****

A great relationship doesn't happen because
of the love you had in the beginning but how
well you continue building on love till the end.
Love is beautiful when it lasts.

#ShazSays

It's always exciting when we start a new relationship - the honeymoon phase as they call it. Everything is beautiful during this time. We understand each other. We enjoy each other's company. Then things start getting real. Suddenly we see things we don't quite like about our partner. Love is awesome when you continue to make an effort everyday to build on it.

****

Don't get upset over lost time because a million wrongs will lead you to the right one.

#ShazSays

We have been in and out of love several
times. At times we even reflect and beat
ourselves over the time we think we wasted in
those failed relationships. Take heart. All
those wrongs will eventually lead you to the
right one.

****

Just be done and walk away from anyone or anything that no longer matches your desires.

#ShazSays

Don't keep holding on to a relationship that's no longer working for you simply because it's the norm you're used to. Be strong enough to walk away. It is pointless being with someone you're no longer happy with and miss an opportunity to meet someone new.

****

Infatuation is sweet but it ain't love. Sexual chemistry ain't love either; don't get it twisted.

#ShazSays

Many times, we find ourselves staying in a relationship with someone simply because the sex is great. At the back of our minds we know very well that this ain't going anywhere but then we think about the sex… Love is more than just about that. Love is not infatuation either. Infatuation drives you to flings. Love drives you to something deeper.

****

You give attention to what you enjoy or love;
rest assured they do the same too.

#ShazSays

I have seen many people make excuses for their partners who no longer make an effort to spend time with them. You'll hear them say, "he's busy these days" etc. But I will guarantee you this, he will be making time to be with his friends or even someone new! There are no excuses.

****

You need to know yourself first for you to know what it is you want from a relationship.

#ShazSays

Several times people just get into relationships for the sake of it. They don't even know what they want. Matter of fact, they don't know themselves well enough to know what they really want. So, when they are presented with stuff they don't even like, they accept them. The relationship carries on like this until they get frustrated.

****

There's a difference between love and lust.
Don't fall for anything less than love.

#ShazSays

Lust is more sexual than anything. It doesn't see the beauty of a person beyond their physical appearance. Therefore, its satisfaction is physically driven. Love on the other hand, looks at the physical and beyond. While physical appearance is crucial, love also looks at the beauty inside a person. Now that's something worth going for.

****

You can be your absolute worst and yet be
perfect for the right one.

#ShazSays

During a break up, if you're lucky enough, your partner will tell you the reasons they want to break up with you. These reasons vary. When the relationship finally ends, and you meet someone new, then boom! They love you even with all those flaws! Wow! This doesn't mean that they don't see the flaws but simply that they want you regardless.

****

Fall in love. Capture moments and enjoy each
day like there's no tomorrow.

#ShazSays

Life is for living so live!

****

Yes, love with all you've got but take care of
your heart in the process. Turn away from the
things that constantly hurt you.

#ShazSays

Have you ever stayed in a relationship with someone who no longer loved you and all they did was just hurtful? Well, you're not the only one. However, you can free yourself from that undeserved pain - it's not worth it. There is someone better out there.

****

Finding love and friendship in one person -
nothing beats that!

#ShazSays

There are times when the things happening in our relationship weigh us down. It's moments like these (and more) that we actually need the friend in our partner. Their friendship will carry us through it all.

****

Watch your relationships. Don't keep investing in a bankrupt system - it will leave you empty.

#ShazSays

In any relationship, the give and take system should be at play. If you keep pouring yourself out with nobody refilling you, then soon or later, you'll find yourself empty. Be weary of people who suck you dry.

****

Ain't nothing like the smile of a happy woman!

#ShazSays

A lot of times, as women, we have allowed our worlds to revolve around men. We feel as though we are incomplete without them. This is a lie and we should not believe it. We are beautiful and complete all by ourselves. There's a certain level of beauty that is carried by a happy woman. Even when she smiles, that smile makes her even more beautiful. Be happy in yourself and by yourself.

****

Admit when you're wrong. Don't let your ego
make you loyal to your mistakes.

#ShazSays

There will be conflict in any relationship.
When that phase hits your relationship,
remember that it's not about who's right or
wrong. Let it be about finding a solution that
works for both of you. It's not about winning
an argument. It's all about resolving issues.

****

Lock the world away and enjoy quality time…
Simple things count.

#ShazSays

These days there's so much a couple can do in doors; Netflix and chill. Invest in moments like this. Thank me later.

****

Don't get trapped in an unhappy relationship -
walk away!

#ShazSays

Believe me, it is better to deal with the pain of
recovery than that of ambivalence,
indifference or looking the other way.

****

Don't rush relationships but don't settle for
situationships either.

#ShazSays

When you meet someone new, and you're getting to know each other before the actual relationship begins, don't rush anything. At the same time, don't allow this slow pace to make you settle for a little thrill. You deserve better.

****

Conflict resolution is key in any relationship - maturity and respect are its centerpiece. Remember, drama gives no upper hand.

#ShazSays

It's not about who's wrong and who's right but more about what's wrong and what's right. Even when fighting, avoid crossing over to calling each other names. Also avoid all the drama that may come along with conflict. Keep respect and maturity as the centerpiece of it all.

****

There's a difference between loving someone and not wanting to spend the rest of your life without them.

#ShazSays

This, I believe, is where marriage or not comes to play. You can be in a relationship with someone and actually love each other. The relationship can go for years and be good. Then one day, it ends. Your partner meets someone new and they waste no time getting married. This simply means that they now found someone they did not want to live the rest of their lives without.

****

Lose the fear and take a chance. Love is beautiful.

#ShazSays

Shola Ama puts it beautifully in her song Still Believe. No matter how many times we have been hurt in relationships, keep your hope in love alive.

****

Forget the busy schedule and be playful.

#ShazSays

At times you just need to let loose! Go on that road trip. Take that vacation. Stay indoors all day. Go fishing. Play games. Just let loose and enjoy your love.

****

You can't get the relationship you need from someone who's not ready to give it to you. Let them go. Some chapters just have to close even without closure.

ShazSays

Things change in relationships a lot of times. Some change is good. Some change, though, may leave us broken and hurt. You can be in a long-term relationship with someone then you start desiring marriage commitment from them - something that they won't be ready to give. Don't keep holding on because it will only hurt you. Don't fall in the trap of holding on in search of closure. Just move on.

****

In and out of love, make love jams the
rhythm of your heart.

#ShazSays

Love jams, (not the sad ones) have a way of reviving your faith in love. They will continue to paint a beautiful picture of love. Keep them playing.

****

Don't let the game of love change you; stay true to yourself. You are beautiful just the way you are.

#ShazSays

A lot of the times we are left brokenhearted, we vow to never love again and yet, that's not what we really want. Some resort to cheating after being cheated on. Don't let the game change you. Simply change the people you attract.

****

They say keep fighting and keep holding on.
Well, I just think that something worth
holding on to would not have let go.

#ShazSays

In an attempt to fix your broken relationship, don't fight for someone who is ready and willing to let go. You can't change their mind. Nothing but more pain will come out of this.

****

Don't question if you were not enough. The problem is you were so enough they couldn't handle it. It's their loss.

#ShazSays

At times our self-esteem is left messed up
after a breakup and we find ourselves
wondering whether or not we were enough.
Truth of the matter is, we were and are
enough. We were just with the wrong person.

****

Don't be wooed by a man's appearance or title. Rather, choose a man whose mind and spirit court yours.

#ShazSays

Love is more than just what we see on the surface; it's deep. While the physical aspect is important, forget not the emotional and mental - that's what defines a person.

****

Do not allow his words to pierce your soul.
Instead, open your mind to something new -
it is always better.

#ShazSays

No matter how many times breakups occur,
never allow them to steal your hope in love.
Some partners can be so abusive and hurtful.
Take time to heal after a relationship with
such.

****

Never run back to what broke you.
Remember, they are an ex for a reason.

#ShazSays

Many of us are guilty of this error. Some of these hook-ups with our exes emanate from wanting to see if there is something left there. The relationship ended - that's the fact that remains and should keep us from giving into the curiosity of wanting to find out whether or not we could kick it again.

****

Love yourself.

#ShazSays

I truly believe that you cannot love someone before you learn how to love yourself. You cannot give what you don't have.

The importance of loving yourself, as well, is that it helps you escape the danger of tolerating nonsense. So yes, love yourself.

****

You are not defined by your partner's appreciation of you or the lack of it thereof. You are complete and enough all by yourself.

#ShazSays

Sometimes we find ourselves desperately trying to please the other. It's ok to want to make your partner happy. Just don't lose yourself in doing so. And when they're not satisfied even after all your effort, don't think of yourself any less.

****

Think twice about being with someone who
does not asseverate their love for you.

#ShazSays

A partner who truly loves you or wants you will make it clear that they love you and want you in their life. They will profess their love for you and show it in ways you won't even doubt. Be with such a partner.

****

Do not allow memories of good times to keep you committed to a relationship that no longer serves you. Consistency is a fundamental element of love.

#ShazSays

There are a lot of reasons why people hold on to relationships. Holding on to the good memories can be one such reason. Sadly, memories of a great past are not enough to fix the present. Move on.

****

Nobody should make you feel unworthy by withholding love. Be the first to love yourself.

#ShazSays

I have seen some women stay in relationships with men who made it so clear, through their actions, that they didn't want them anymore. Walk away from such relationships before they break the core of who you are.

****

In your relationship, master your roles. Do not allow the world to mess that up.

#ShazSays

It is not old fashioned. We were designed to play certain roles in life. Master your role in a relationship. Discuss these roles with your partner and play the part. Your relationship will function better.

****

Be with someone whose intentions match
your desires.

#ShazSays

It's important to know what it is you want from a relationship before you even get into one. There's a danger of accepting whatever is offered if you do not know or state what exactly you want.

****

One up for love!

#ShazSays

145

Let us celebrate the gift of love!

****

HEADS UP!

Many couples secretly struggle with their marriages and desperately want to save them, but they fail dismally. If your marriage is on a decline and you fear the possibility of divorce, Sharon and her partner, Brian, are available to help. To get started, contact Sharon on: SharonMukuze@gmail.com

ABOUT THE AUTHOR

Sharon Mukuze is a passionate love junkie who loves as if she has never been loved before. She lives in South Africa with her two children. When not writing, her work involves helping children and women affected by shame and low self-esteem to create and to live their best lives.

She is also an affluent love coach and speaks to women and couples from all walks of life. In her seminars, she seeks to point her participants towards the true kind of love, as it ought to be.

Sharon and her partner, Brian, help couples resolve marital conflict.